A Special Gift for

_____

with love,

_____

date

_____

DOG LOVERS

Stories, sayings, and scriptures to Encourage and Inspire

hugs ™

for
Dog
Lovers

WILLIE & KORIE ROBERTSON

Personalized Scriptures by
LEANN WEISS

HOWARD BOOKS
A DIVISION OF SIMON & SCHUSTER
New York   London   Toronto   Sydney

For **Sadie,** who patiently practices her mothering skills on her little brother and sister

For **Will,** whose fun and playful spirit fills our home and hearts

For **Bella,** who
brightens each day
with her smile

For **John Luke,** who
opened our eyes to the love
of animals

Our purpose at Howard Books is to:
- *Increase* faith in the hearts of growing Christians
- *Inspire* holiness in the lives of believers
- *Instill* hope in the hearts of struggling people everywhere

Because He's coming again!

HOWARD
BOOKS

Published by Howard Books, a division of Simon & Schuster, Inc.
1230 Avenue of the Americas, New York, NY 10020
www.howardpublishing.com

Hugs for Dog Lovers © 2007 by Willie & Korie Robertson

Paraphrased scriptures © 2007 by LeAnn Weiss
3006 Brandywine Drive, Orlando, FL 32806
407-898-4410

10 Digit ISBN: 1-58229-666-9; 13 Digit ISBN: 978-1-58229-666-1
10 Digit ISBN: 1-4165-3580-2; 13 Digit ISBN: 978-1-4165-3580-5

10 9 8 7 6 5 4 3 2 1

For information regarding special discounts for bulk purchases, please contact Simon & Schuster Special Sales at 1-800-456-6798 or business@simonandschuster.com.

Edited by Between the Lines
Cover design by John Mark Luke Designs
Interior design by John Mark Luke Designs

Contents

1

Your Dog,
a Partner

1

Look up and remember that your help comes from Me. I am for you! You can do all things because I strengthen you. Nothing can ever separate you from My amazing love! Whatever your difficulty or obstacle, with My help you will triumph.

Helping you,

Your Heavenly Father

—FROM PSALM 121:1–2; PHILIPPIANS 4:13; ROMANS 8:31, 35–37

3

What makes a dog such a good friend? Could it be that dogs don't care about the things that seem to matter so much to humans? They don't even notice how much money you make or what kind of car you drive. They love you whether you were the vale-dictorian of your senior class or you finished somewhere near the bottom. They accept and value you whether you were the homecoming queen or the class clown.

Your dog is always there for you—whether you won the account that would make your company a huge sum of money or you forgot to make the call and lost the deal. Whether you're still happily married to your high-school sweetheart or you've just been through a painful divorce.

Have you ever heard your dog spreading the latest gossip? Did he treat you differently after you lost your job? Has she made fun of you because you've put on a few extra pounds?

Of course not, and here's why: a dog's love comes without conditions. Above all else, dogs are accepting and loyal. How wonderful to have a friend that loves you and is there for you on your good days as well as your bad. Do you ever wish you had more friends like that? Have you ever wished you could be a friend like that? Your relationship with your dog can be one of your most rewarding. You can have—and be—a loving, loyal partner.

We give dogs **time** we can spare, space

we can spare, and **love** we can spare.

And in return, dogs give us their **all**.

M. Facklam

It was a beautiful, strong dog that Mattie had painted, but somehow Cheryl sensed both strength and sadness in the dog's eyes and recognized her daughter's reflection.

Snapshots

"Smile," Cheryl pleaded, trying to sound cheerful. She snapped a picture of her daughter. The beautiful little girl stood sad and alone in front of the flag—in stark contrast to the festively adorned school gym. Each year it was the same. The awards ceremony and celebration on the last day of school was never the fun, special day it should be—the way it was for other kids.

Most girls in the class were busy hugging each other, saying their good-byes, and making plans to play together throughout the summer. Some proudly held or showed off the achievement awards they'd just won. But Mattie stood empty-handed—just as she had the year before . . . and the year before that. Standing quietly to the side, Mattie looked at the floor and fidgeted awkwardly with her empty hands.

Mattie never won any achievement awards. Those weren't given to the child who had barely passed third grade and was still having difficulty reading. The teachers had finally identified the learning disability that was making school so difficult for nine-year-old Mattie, but that hadn't improved the way other kids treated her or the way she felt about herself.

"I think you did great, honey," Cheryl encouraged her daughter, smoothing the little girl's hair in a protective, motherly gesture. Mattie smiled bravely, but she didn't look convinced.

"You know, your dad and I are very proud of you whether you got an award or not." Cheryl wished she could wave a magic wand to make it all better. She and her husband, Brandon, knew their daughter was smart, sweet, and kind. They just couldn't seem to find an arena in which she could succeed. Scholastics wasn't it, and they'd tried music, sports, and drama—all without success. It was evident that Mattie's self-esteem was suffering.

Mattie never asked permission for friends to come home after school and was never invited to other girls' houses. She spent much of her time alone, playing in her room, daydreaming, and drawing.

Cheryl and Brandon each took one of Mattie's hands and walked with her one last time to her classroom to thank the teacher and gather Mattie's supplies and papers to take home. Cheryl's eye was drawn to a beautiful painting of a running dog displayed on the art wall. She was surprised and pleased to see that it was Mattie's work. Technically, it seemed superior to the other kids' pictures of houses, schools, people, and cars. But what most stood out to Cheryl was the feeling Mattie had captured. The brown, longhaired dog ran alone. It was a beautiful, strong dog that Mattie had painted, but somehow Cheryl sensed both strength and sadness in the dog's eyes and recognized her daughter's reflection.

Cheryl had to suppress a gasp. In a moment she'd glimpsed Mattie's spirit in the image of the dog: struggling against feelings of worthlessness; trying as hard as she could not to show how alone she really felt, wanting to run, unable to escape the prison of her disabilities; alone.

Cheryl resolved to find a way to help her daughter truly smile again.

Cheryl didn't have to tell Mattie to smile as she snapped her daughter's picture hugging the tiny collie pup. Mattie's ear-to-ear grin hadn't left her face since the moment she saw her dad carrying her very special birthday present into the living room.

Mattie's mouth had dropped, eyes practically popping out of her head, and a squeal of sheer delight let Cheryl and Brandon know exactly how successful their gift was. Mattie hugged both her parents tightly.

"What are you going to name him?" Cheryl asked.

"You mean, I get to name him?" exclaimed Mattie.

Her father chuckled. "Well, of course, you do—he's yours."

"The owner says this one was the runt of the litter and has had a few health problems," Cheryl warned her infatuated daughter. "So don't expect him to get as big as other—"

"I don't care," Mattie interrupted, admiring her new dog's adorable face and smooth brown and white coat. "I think he's perfect." She looked straight into her puppy's eyes. "Rocky, you're absolutely the most beautiful dog in the whole world."

"Rocky . . . I like it," Brandon announced. "And when he's old enough, there's a kennel club down the road. You could take him to their classes."

Mattie was hardly listening. She pressed her cheek against Rocky's soft fur with an expression of love. The small puppy licked her face and made soft sounds in return, gently responding to the young girl. "Hey, he likes me!" Mattie cried with surprised delight.

Cheryl and Brandon stood with arms around each other. Cheryl's eyes were filled with tears, and she could tell Brandon was battling a lump in his throat. Cheryl had a good feeling—and a whole lot of hope—that this little collie would be just what their daughter needed.

Cheryl stood, camera in hand, waiting for the crowd to die down so she could snap another picture of the prize-winning show dog and his proud owner. Mattie looked beautiful in the dress Cheryl had made for her daughter's special day.

The competition had just ended with Mattie and Rocky circling the arena, certificate proclaiming "Best in Show" in Mattie's hand. Over the past few years, Rocky had become just that.

Mattie's entire class had turned out to see their friend compete in the AKC Junior Showmanship event. "We're all here!" she heard Mattie's teacher announce proudly. Cheryl knew the teacher had spread the word and organized the seventh-graders to come watch their friend at this special competition. Mattie's classmates pushed exuberantly to the front of the arena to congratulate the young star on her latest victory.

"Wow, you were great!" Cheryl heard a girl in Mattie's class exclaim with enthusiasm.

"Could I have your autograph?" a boy asked shyly.

Cheryl and Brandon couldn't have been more thrilled for their daughter. The shy, self-conscious girl from just three years before was long gone. Cheryl knew that much of the credit for Mattie's turnaround belonged to Rocky.

A low whistle of appreciation broke Cheryl's reverie and made her aware of a man standing at her left elbow. It was Mr. Cooper, the collie breeder.

"They make a great team," Cheryl said. "They seem to bring out the best in each other." She kept her eyes on Mattie, who, in spite of all the commotion and adulation, lovingly leaned down to gently kiss the canine friend she adored.

"I can't believe that's the little runt I sold you," Cooper said, shaking his head. "I never thought he could be a champion."

"Mattie believed in him," Cheryl said, with tears of joy moistening the corners of her eyes. "Sometimes that's all it takes."

"I guess so." Cooper nodded agreeably. "If I'd have known he'd turn out this good, I never would have sold him to you—at least not so cheap." He smiled and winked.

Brandon put his arm around his wife's waist, and they

watched as reporters' cameras flashed brightly and Mattie smiled radiantly and posed alongside her beloved dog. Mattie and Rocky exuded strength and confidence.

Cheryl dabbed away happy tears and raised her camera. This was a snapshot she didn't want to miss.

2

Your Dog, a Teacher

In My hand is the life of every creature and the breath of all people. Learn by observing My handiwork in the animals, the birds, nature, and the fish. I'll instruct you and teach you in the way you should go. I'll counsel you and watch over you.

Guiding you,

Your Creator

—FROM JOB 12:7–10; PSALM 32:8

19

Have you ever seen yourself in your dog? Perhaps you've noticed this strange phenomenon: after a period of being together, people and the dogs they love often start to look alike. You may even have discussed it around the dinner table with your family. Maybe that bulldog didn't look like your uncle Fritz when he first joined the family, but after years together, everyone begins to wonder if he's not a long-lost brother.

Or perhaps we choose the animals that look like us physically or share common personality traits. You may have known the chatty, older lady who bought herself a talkative terrier, or the soft-spoken girl who adores her gentle English toy spaniel. You've probably seen the active little boy who spends every waking moment outside running and jumping with his energetic puppy. You might even be the strong-willed, independent girl with the adventuresome, slightly stubborn Siberian Husky.

Sometimes we learn about ourselves through our animals. Could it be that your dog is in your home to teach you something or to help you grow—to show you something about yourself you might never have seen otherwise? Who can say how we'll learn our next lessons in life—and who will be our teacher?

God teaches us things through all of His creation. Sometimes He uses the tiniest, gentlest, least likely of His creatures to fulfill His great purpose in our lives. Don't look past your puppy; pay attention. You just might learn something.

Dogs have given us their **absolute** all.

We are the center of their universe.

We are the **focus** of their love and faith

and trust. They **serve** us in return

for scraps. It is without a doubt the

best deal man has ever made.

Roger Caras

For the first time she was able to
see clearly the kind of love her
mother had told her about.

Love Lessons

"Leave me alone!" fourteen-year-old Alexis sputtered angrily. "I never want to speak to you again!" she shouted at her stricken mother. She slammed the bedroom door, narrowly avoiding hitting her dog, Princess, as she streaked into the room.

It only took a few minutes for Alexis's mother to appear outside the door, knocking quietly but with determination.

"Go away," Alexis warned grumpily as she plopped down on her bed.

"Alexis, don't do this to me." Her mother's voice was a mixture of pleading and warning. "I'm your mother. I love you . . . but you're hurting me."

Good, Alexis thought but was too smart or too kind to say. Part of her was glad that someone else was feeling as miserable as she was since her parents' divorce. Part of her felt self-satisfaction that she had the power to make someone else suffer after so prolonged a period when she'd felt helpless to stop her own suffering.

Another part of Alexis felt guilty—she knew the divorce wasn't really her mother's fault. She even suspected that she was taking out her own feelings of anger toward her father against her mother—the one within striking distance. But the suspicion didn't really matter. The anger and pain inside just had to come out. And her mom could be so . . . *annoying*, among other things.

"If you really loved me, you wouldn't hassle me all the time . . . about my friends . . . about when I come home . . . about everything!" Alexis snarled through the door.

There was a pained silence from the other side. "I *do* love you, Alexis," her mother said slowly. "When I express concern about your friends and your behavior, I *am* showing love."

"It doesn't feel like love," Alexis said with calculated firmness. "Is this how you loved Dad?" Alexis knew she'd scored a direct hit. The silence on the other side of the door was total. Her mother was gone.

Feeling truly alone, Alexis pondered her last words. Her mother had told her many times that she loved her, but she had heard her parents say that to each other before. She rolled onto her back, taking in her eclectic mix of posters and a few pictures of friends and of her family—back when they *were* a family.

It made her sad to look at the picture of her with her mom and dad on their trip to the beach, taken just weeks before they had given her the news. Her dad had been so calm about it, like it was nothing—"Oh yeah, by the way, your mother and I won't be living together anymore"—like Alexis's whole life was not going to change forever with that one sentence.

After the court hearing that gave her mom full custody, Alexis and her mom had sat down and talked. Her mother had assured Alexis that even though she and her father were not together anymore, nothing would ever change the way she felt about her only daughter. She had said that she loved Alexis—that no matter what Alexis went through, no matter what she would face in these difficult teenage years—her love for her would never falter.

Her mom had spoken of the love God has for His children—unconditional love that knows no limits or end. "You can't separate yourself from that kind of love, Alexis, and that's the kind of love I have for you."

But the current situation made Alexis feel unsettled. She certainly hadn't been the easiest person to live with this past year. Could her mom's love hold up in spite of the horrible, hurtful things Alexis had so often said to her? What had made her parents stop loving each other? Couldn't that same thing happen to their love for her?

Alexis tried to wade through her tumultuous thoughts and feelings as she lay on her bed. Suddenly she felt a soft, warm tongue on her arm. "Go away, Princess," Alexis said irritably. But Princess only increased the speed of her licking. "I mean it!" she shouted harshly. "That's gross! Leave me alone!"

She pulled her hand away, but Princess followed, undaunted, wagging her tail in a friendly and appealing manner. Alexis steeled herself against the urge to respond to Princess's show of affection, unwilling to let go of her anger and self-pity. Roughly, she pushed Princess away, then turned away from her. But by the slight movement of the bed, Alexis knew Princess had returned and was wagging her tail fiercely, trying even harder to make up with her unhappy mistress. Alexis ignored her for a minute . . . then two . . . then three. The wagging continued, and then Princess started making little noises—first an *"urf"*—like a small sneeze to politely get her attention. That was followed by low conciliatory vocalizations that Alexis knew were the little dog's way of pleading for things to be right.

Doesn't this dog ever give up? Without condescending even to look at Princess, Alexis swung her arm around and swept the dog roughly off the bed. Alexis simultaneously felt a sense of power and guilt for the impact she was having on Princess. But then Princess was there again—in her face, licking, then pressing into her body, trying to burrow affectionately under Alexis.

What does it take to get through to this dog? She scooped up the little poodle, carried her to the door, and tossed her outside before slamming the door shut. "Don't you get it?" she practically screamed. "Leave me alone!"

Alexis flopped back down on the bed, fuming. "Dumb dog," she muttered. "What do I have to do to get you to leave me alone?"

Suddenly Alexis felt a stab of fear in her heart. What would she do if Princess ever did "get it" and left her alone for good? She realized she couldn't stand the thought of having pushed everyone away and being totally alone. She bounded up from the bed and to the door. She desperately needed to go after Princess and restore their broken relationship. "Princess," she called, flinging open the door. "Princess—*oomph*—" Alexis tripped over the tiny form crouched at the doorway; the dog's nose must have been practically under the door.

"Princess," she cooed affectionately, scooping up the little dog and showering her head with kisses. "How can you ever forgive me?" But the squirmy, warm response reassured Alexis that she already had. She let Princess lick her cheek. "You didn't go away . . . even when I told you to. I just don't get it."

Just then a light went on in Alexis's head. She was push-
ing her mom away just like she had pushed away the little
dog—the dog who had only wanted to be with Alexis, show
her love, and make things better for her. Was that the way
her mother felt about her too?

For the first time she was able to see clearly the kind of
love her mother had told her about. Arguments, harsh words,
fear, and resentment had drowned out those words over the
past year, but now, standing there in the hall, Alexis suddenly heard them loud and clear. They spoke to her heart
and set her free. She had been afraid her mother would stop
loving her, but she never would. Alexis didn't have to test
that love, prove it, or push it away for fear of being hurt
when she lost it. Her mother would always love her—no
matter what. How had she not seen it before? That's what
her mother had been telling—no, showing—her all along.

The young girl cried for a while, wondering how to mend
the fences, to tear down the walls she had been building
brick by brick for so long. Then slowly she moved down the
hallway, carrying the dog that had taught her the lesson a

thousand words hadn't fully communicated. Princess quietly rubbed her face into Alexis's chest as though she understood the significance of the moment. Alexis would make things right with her mother.

She found her lying on the bed in her own room, gazing up at her ceiling in the same pose Alexis had been in just moments before. It was clear she had been crying.

Alexis handed Princess to her mother as one would hand over a peace offering, then lay down on the bed at her mother's side. "I love you," she whispered as she grasped her mother's hand.

Her mother turned to look at Alexis, a mixture of hope and shock in her red-rimmed eyes. "I love you too," she said with great feeling and gratitude. Then, repeating those simple words, Alexis's mother held her daughter tightly and tenderly kissed her cheek. "I'll always love you."

Alexis pulled away only slightly, so she could look into her mother's eyes. "I know, Mom." She gave a sidelong glance and a smile in Princess's direction. "I finally get it."

3

Your Dog, a Protector

I am your refuge and your strength. I'm your ever-present help in times of trouble. My name is your strong tower of protection. The righteous run to Me and are safe. Give Me all your worries, and I'll sustain you. I won't let you fall. I'll command My angels concerning you, to guard you in all your ways.

Protecting hugs,
The Lord Your God

—FROM PSALM 46:1; PROVERBS 18:10; PSALMS 55:22; 91:11

Is your dog your protector? Maybe he didn't pull you from a burning building, or you don't need her to be your "eyes" because you can't see, but your dog can still protect you. In small ways every day, the little things dogs do can help you make it through the difficult times of life.

Maybe you've never thought of it this way, but when your dog is there for you each morning when you wake up, perhaps she's protecting you from the fear of being alone. When he demands that you take him for his daily walk, he may be rescuing you from the stresses of the day. When you feel her warmth at the foot of your bed, she is sheltering you from the coldness of life. When you laugh at his silly antics, he saves you from the sadness that might otherwise creep into your soul. When he reminds you that he's hungry, he keeps you from thinking only of yourself. When she stands at the door—waiting—until you return, she saves you from feeling unappreciated.

Life isn't easy. Sometimes we need someone or something to protect us from the dangers of the world around us—to rescue us when we're drowning in the little things, or even in the things that aren't so little. God knows that. He's there for you, watching out for you, knowing just when you need His protection. Who knows, He may be sending your dog into action just for you!

He is your **friend**, your partner, your defender, your dog. You are his life, his love, his **leader**. He will be yours, faithful and true, to the last **beat** of his heart.

Author Unknown

Mother and son both found comfort
in being able to touch the dog
that had meant so much to their
beloved husband and father.

A Nudge in the Right Direction

3

Katy sat with her elbow on the kitchen table, forehead in the palm of her hand. She shook her head as she surveyed the mound of bills spread out before her, then looked out the window, hoping for some cheery sunshine to brighten her mood. Unfortunately, her view was blocked by a sink piled high with dirty dishes.

Since her husband, Phillip, had died nine months ago, the responsibilities of running the household seemed more than Katy could handle. The older boys would be home from school soon, and she would have to figure out what to do for dinner. She just never seemed able to catch up anymore. The knot in her stomach tightened, and she choked back the tears that threatened to engulf her.

A slurpy tongue on her bare ankles jarred Katy from her discouraged preoccupation. "Oh, Gabe," she said with an emotional sigh, bending down to wrap her arms around the chocolate Labrador retriever. "You have a way of knowing just when I need a little TLC." Tears were on the verge of spilling onto her cheeks when two of the boys arrived home from school. Even in the worst of times, Katy marveled at the gift of her children. Their deep dimples marked them unmistakably as their father's sons.

Jared strode into the kitchen with all the confidence of a firstborn. He flipped his sun-streaked hair out of his eyes and kissed her lightly on the cheek. "What can I do to help?"

I should be asking you that question, Katy thought, then smiled. She grabbed him for a big hug, amazed at how he always seemed to know when she was under too much stress.

Jonathan, her serious eight-year-old, plopped down on the chair beside her with a scowl that seemed to have become a permanent fixture. He was taking his father's death the hardest.

"How was school?" Katy asked hopefully.

A Nudge in the Right Direction

"All right," Jonathan mumbled. Short, bleak answers were about all Katy was able to extract from her middle child these days.

Jonathan ran his fingers through Gabe's fur, and Katy noticed with relief that this simple contact was slowly lightening her son's mood. Gabe seemed to have the same effect on Jonathan as he did on her. Mother and son both found comfort in being able to touch the dog that had meant so much to their beloved husband and father.

Katy's mind drifted back to the early days with their dog. Phillip had been an avid sportsman and had purchased Gabe to train as a hunting dog. She smiled as she remembered her husband's funny tales of the active pup who would rather play with the hunters than chase the ducks. Phillip had quickly given up on training Gabe, and Gabe had become the family pet—a role the dog seemed to relish. He spent his days faithfully retrieving sticks, guarding the back door, and sleeping on the front porch of their country home.

Katy leaned over and took Gabe's furry face in her hands. She peered into his eyes, trying to send a message of gratitude for being the one constant in her life when everything else had been turned upside down. A lick on the hand was his reply, and Katy accepted it as a "You're welcome." Security was what she needed now, and Gabe, in his unassuming way, was up to the challenge.

Katy looked up to see her youngest son, Jake, toddle in from the playroom. "Jon-Jon! Jarey!" he yelled, grabbing each of his brothers at the knees. They gave him a pat on the head and headed for the refrigerator. Jake went with them, recognizing an opportunity for a snack. At two and a half, he wasn't quite big enough to get anything for himself, although he often tried. Katy and the older boys had gotten used to Jake's battle cry of "No, me!" whenever they tried to perform a task for him that he felt quite sure he could handle on his own.

Jake was a whirlwind of activity, but most days Katy was grateful to have her "little tornado" around the house. His smiles—and his messes—gave her mind a break from the frequent instant replays she still saw of Phillip's battered car.

Katy rose wearily from her chair and poured drinks for

the boys. Today performing even this smallest of motherly duties was difficult.

"Why don't you guys go outside for a while?" she suggested to Jared and Jonathan. "Jake would love for you to play with him, and Gabe could use the exercise."

"OK, Mom," Jared responded, always eager to please.

"Keep your eye on Jake," she reminded them as they closed the back door. "He can't swim yet."

"I'll try," Jared yelled over his shoulder.

The lake that had been appealing when she and Phillip had bought this house had proven to be a mixed blessing. It did offer some peace and tranquility: as she looked out her window each morning to a sunrise that cast beautiful shadows on smooth water, she often was reminded that God can calm any storm. Still, until Jake learned to swim, the lake would also be a constant source of worry.

Only minutes later Jared and Jonathan returned with a tearful Jake. "Mom, he won't stay with us," Jared said, exasperated. "And me and Jonathan want to play computer games." But sensing his mom's disappointment, he quickly recanted: "Never mind—we can watch him a little longer."

"No, it's fine, you guys go play." Katy knew the older boys needed time to themselves without a little brother always tagging along. "I'll see if Jake will sit down for a movie." She hated to use the television as a baby-sitter, but she had work to do, and it seemed no matter how hard she tried these days, she always found something to feel guilty about.

Katy settled Jake in front of the TV with his favorite video and resumed her unpleasant task at the kitchen table. Gabe rejoined her, flopping down on the tile at her feet. He was wet and panting from retrieving tennis balls the boys had thrown into the lake.

"Oh well, it was fun while it lasted, wasn't it, boy? Thanks for playing with them," she whispered affectionately.

A few moments later Gabe got up and lumbered to the door. *He must be hungry or thirsty from all the playing,* Katy thought as she watched him go through the pet door Phillip had installed.

Halfway through the stack of bills, Katy felt a sudden

uneasiness. The house was too quiet. She went to the play-room to check on Jake. He was gone!

Her heart sank just as it had the night she opened the door to greet the state trooper. She ran to the front entry-way. Only a few days before, she had realized that Jake had learned to turn the knob and open the door. She arrived to find her fears confirmed. The door was standing wide open.

Terrified, Katy raced outside. Her worst nightmare sped through her frantic mind as she sprinted to the back of the house, knowing Jake would head straight for the lake. Pray-ing desperately that she would catch her little one in time, she turned the corner and came in view of the water. Her breath caught in her throat, and giant tears formed as she slowed, then stopped.

She didn't need to go any farther. There was Gabe, the family's loyal, loving dog, patiently nudging her youngest son toward the house. They were already halfway home. Katy shuddered to think how long this astonishing act of protection had gone on without her realizing it. Each time her headstrong toddler turned in the direction of the lake,

Gabe blocked his path by putting his nose to Jake's side and gently guided him in the direction of safety.

Katy waited at the top of the hill, allowing Gabe to complete the job he had started. When they reached her, she hugged them both. Unaware of his recent danger, Jake wriggled to free himself from her grasp while Gabe, more receptive to her embrace, tried to dry off on her clean blouse.

Katy picked up Jake and, holding him tightly, walked back to the house with Gabe following proudly behind. Now, as she entered the kitchen, the stack of bills seemed smaller. The pile of dishes didn't look nearly as high. Her heart felt lighter, free of the burdens that had troubled her just moments before.

That evening after dinner, Jared and Jonathan did their homework while Katy tucked Jake into bed and went to the sink to clean up. As she looked out the window, moonlight shimmered on some fading ripples on the lake. "Thank You, God," she whispered as tears of relief flooded her eyes. She knew He had used Gabe to protect their family from another tragedy . . . and that He would indeed calm this storm.

4

Your Dog, a Comforter

No matter what you're experiencing in life, even in the middle of life-and-death, earth-shattering situations, you don't have to fear. I'm with you, flooding you with comfort in all of your troubles so you can reach out to others. As a mother comforts her child, I will lovingly comfort you.

Loving you,

Your God of All Comfort

—from Psalm 23:4; 2 Corinthians 1:3–7; Isaiah 66:13

Have you ever noticed that pets seem especially treasured by the really young and the really old?

As we grow older, our dogs often become our company and our comfort. Perhaps you've had a taste of this if you've ever felt alone or sad, and the dog who's been there for you through life's ups and downs sits at your feet or crawls onto your lap, listening attentively as you talk, offering his own special brand of therapy.

Kids have a special bond with pets too. They don't think about the time it takes to house-train or feed a puppy. They just know their furry friends are there when they're hurting. A child will throw his arms around the broad, soft neck of a dog and let his tears fall into the woe-absorbing fur.

Somewhere between childhood and retirement, many of us get too busy to enjoy the benefits a dog can bring. But at any age there are extra blessings to be found when we slow down a little and love our canine friends. We rediscover the comfort in their company. So why wait? Embrace it now. Talk to your dog all you want, even if you look a little silly. Look into his eyes, cry, and hug him when you're feeling blue. Feel your stress ebb away with each stroke of her fur. And cherish your dog. You'll feel better before you know it.

There is no psychiatrist in the world
like a puppy licking your face.

Bern Williams

Never again would Mel's
face be the last thing she
saw at night or the first
one she saw upon waking.

Missing Mel

Merritt awoke with an unsettled feeling of dread. Where was she? What was this place? It was nighttime, and she was in bed, but even without her glasses she could tell the shadows were wrong—ominous. This wasn't home.

Was she visiting her son Kenny's family? No. Too many noises . . . lights in the hallway . . . unfamiliar voices in the next room.

"Mel?" she called out hopefully, groping fruitlessly in the darkness, grasping nothing. "Mel?" she echoed softer, uncertainly. She drew her wrinkled hand back to cover her trembling mouth. She could barely suppress a sob as the awful truth came flooding into her consciousness.

Oh, no! This wasn't Kenny and Sarah's place. She wasn't

just visiting. She couldn't just pack up her things and go home tomorrow. She no longer had a home. She was in . . . in . . . that place. That place you went when you weren't quite done with life—but it was done with you.

Merritt turned on her side, buried her face in the pillow, and cried. She felt abandoned—utterly and hopelessly alone. She thought of Mel, but instead of bringing her peace, thoughts of him made her heart ache and her stomach feel hollow. Never again would Mel's face be the last thing she saw at night or the first one she saw upon waking. Never again would his rhythmic, deep breaths close beside her lull her peacefully to sleep. Never again would she feel—

"Mrs. Henning?" Merritt's thoughts were interrupted by a woman's soft, kind-sounding voice and a gentle knocking on her door. Caught off guard, uncertain and embarrassed, Merritt said nothing, but she instantly ceased her crying.

"Mrs. Henning," the voice said again as the door opened and light streamed in from the hall. "Are you all right?"

Merritt lay perfectly still as though she were sleeping, but through one eye opened barely a crack, she could just make out the fuzzy, large, dark shape she recognized as Nurse Rose.

"Mrs. Henning," Rose continued in a concerned voice hardly above a whisper, "I know you're having a rough time adjusting to being here. Woodlawn's a great care center, but it's sure not home."

Merritt continued to listen silently but with rapt attention as Rose sat in the chair beside the bed and leaned close, like an old friend or family member.

"I heard you calling out for your husband," Rose said sympathetically. "I hear you calling every night." She paused and reached for Merritt's hand, squeezing it gently but communicating empathy.

"My husband?" Merritt finally spoke, confused. "You mean James?"

Now Rose sounded confused. "I thought your husband's name was Mel."

Merritt laughed with genuine humor. "My husband, James, was a wonderful man. We had a good life together, and I do miss him." She paused while she sought the right words to express delicately how she felt about James. "But he died almost six years ago."

"Then who's Mel?" Rose asked, perplexed.

"My beautiful, loving . . . cocker spaniel!" Both Merritt and Rose exploded in laughter and shared delight.

Rose gave a low whistle. "That must be some dog," she said with a smile. Merritt nodded and squeezed Rose's hand in agreement. "What happened to him?" Rose asked, almost reverently.

"Nothing happened to him," Merritt said sadly. "It happened to me. I got old. I got sick. I broke my hip. I can't live alone, and I can't ruin my son and daughter-in-law's lives," she sighed. "So here I am . . . cast off and alone while my companion, Mel—my best friend in the world—is shoved in the laundry room all alone at my son Kenny's house." She reclaimed her hand from Rose's grasp to wipe the tears from her eyes.

"I'm so sorry." Rose sounded truly sad for Merritt. "I'm sure your son is taking good care of him," she added, trying to sound encouraging.

Merritt nodded. "Kenny's a good boy. He's trying to do

his best for me—and for Mel. He never complains. But he has two teenagers, and I'm sure they're kind to Mel, but Kenny and his wife both work, and the kids are in school and in sports all day. They can't really understand my silly feelings for a dog—even if he does talk to me . . . and smile on demand. Have you ever seen a dog smile?" Merritt asked Rose. "I promise you, Mel has a beautiful smile." She let out a bittersweet laugh of appreciation tinged with regret.

"Did you ask if you could bring him to live with you here?" Rose inquired helpfully.

"Oh yes," Merritt said bitterly. "But rules are rules. No pets allowed."

"But cocker spaniels are great inside dogs, and I could help take care of him." Rose protested.

"No exceptions," Merritt said. "They told me Mel would be happier with Kenny's family and that I wouldn't have to bother with feeding him and taking him out. But you know, I think I miss that most of all—being responsible for something, caring for someone besides myself, being needed and loved." She started to cry again. "Every night when I went to bed, Mel gave me something to look forward to in the morning." She sniffed and was surprised to hear Rose also sniffling. "I miss him, Rose," she whispered, trying to stifle her sobs. "I miss my Mel."

"Of course you do, honey," Rose said soothingly, patting Merritt's hand. "We may not be able to fight the system around here, but you're not alone, dear," she promised. "Rosie'll sit here with you until you go back to sleep." Grateful for Rose's caring gesture and gentle touch, Merritt settled back into the bed and tried to go to sleep. It would take a long time, that night and for many nights to come.

Merritt awoke from a deep and distant place. Once again the unsettling confusion enveloped her consciousness. The sun was up. It was morning. Where was she? The sad feeling again: this wasn't home. The nursing home? But could that be the sound of a dog barking? Maybe she was home. No, she must be dreaming.

She shook her head to clear the sleepy fog from her brain. It sounded like . . . it couldn't be . . . "Mel?" She fumbled for her glasses and settled them hastily on her face. "Mel?" she echoed hopefully. She looked around the sterile room that still didn't feel like home after nearly a month.

"Mel!" She practically screeched with delight as the energetic cocker spaniel dashed toward her, then launched himself onto her bed. Just like old times—only perhaps a bit more passionately—Mel licked her hand and muzzled her cheek while Merritt hugged him to her and kissed the top of his head.

"How can this be?" Merritt asked, confused. "I don't understand how . . . who . . . Kenny?" she ventured a guess, looking toward the door.

"Kenny's not here," Nurse Rose said mischievously as she leaned against the doorframe. Her broad smile showed off pearly white teeth and dancing dark eyes. She was obviously enjoying the scene before her.

"Then who brought Mel to visit?"

"I did!" Rose chortled triumphantly. "But he's not here to visit," she added before lowering her voice and continuing conspiratorially. "He's working the day shift."

Your Dog, a Comforter

"But the rules . . . ," Merritt protested worriedly.

"The rules say no pets," Rose announced proudly. "But they actually encourage certified pet therapists!" She was practically beaming as she raised her hand to her mouth and whispered, "I certified him myself."

"You won't get in trouble?" Merritt asked, concerned.

"Nah," Rose reassured her. "After our talk the other night, I discussed it with the director. She agreed that a little 'dog therapy' might benefit a lot of the residents around here—if it's OK with you."

"Of course, of course it's OK with me! Mel will certainly cheer things up around here," Merritt said breathlessly as Mel barked excitedly. "But what about Kenny?"

"Kenny and I discussed this, and we agreed this was best for Mel—and for you. I love dogs, and I've got a big old soft spot for cockers—just moved into my own place where I can finally have one. So we worked things out so that Mel will live here—working the day shift—and then I'll take him home for the night shift. You and I will care for him during the day, visiting other residents, cheering up the discouraged, befriending the lonely. He can help lots of people adjust to living here. And the way I'm scheduled pretty much guarantees that you'll be waking up to Mel every morning—just like old times."

Merritt threw her arms around Rose in a poignant, grateful embrace. "Thank you, Rose," she whispered through tears. "I can make it through the night without him, knowing I'll see his adorable face when I wake up in the morning. Thank you for giving me back my comfort and hope. Thank you for giving me back my Mel."

5

Your Dog, a Believer

You can trust in Me with all your heart. Know that I'll direct your steps when you follow Me. I'm loving toward you and faithful in all of My promises to you. My unfailing love surrounds you when you trust in Me!

Faithfully,

Your Trustworthy God

—FROM PROVERBS 3:5–6; PSALMS 145:13; 32:10

The trust between a dog and his or her human is inspiring, if sometimes amusing. Maybe your dog jumps on the end of your bed before the alarm goes off in the morning, because she knows when you wake up, she'll get fed. Perhaps he keeps barking even when you've gone into the next room, because he's sure you can still hear him and will return with a treat—or anything to quiet him while you're on the phone with an important client.

There's nothing like watching a dog's ears perk up at the sound of your voice. She cocks her head as though she understands every word you're saying and believes it's of the utmost importance.

But have you ever bandaged a cut or cleaned out a wound and been amazed at how cooperative and trusting your dog was, even when he couldn't understand what you were doing?

Dogs believe that we love them and will do what's best for them. That we're paying attention when they bark and will somehow understand and meet their needs.

Similarly, we can believe that God loves us and hears us when we talk to Him. First Peter 3:12 says, "The eyes of the Lord are on the righteous and his ears are attentive to their prayer." When you're hurting or in need, just cry out to God—and believe that He's listening.

71

When you **leave** them in the morning, they stick their nose in the door crack and stand there like a **portrait** until you turn the key eight hours later.

Erma Bombeck

Jesse always greeted her when she came home, jumping and barking as if he hadn't seen her in months, even when she'd only been gone for a couple of hours.

Little Dog Lost

5

"We raised him right, Mary, I know we did," Kay said, trying to convince herself more than her friend as they drove home from a day of shopping.

"Of course you did," Mary replied supportively.

"I don't know what to do anymore," Kay confessed. "Nothing makes sense. I can't fix anything. Everything I try to do or say just seems to push Alan further away." Alan was her younger son—the son who had always tested the limits and his parents' rules as he lived life on the edge.

"It's not up to you," Mary said. "You've done all you can. Now you just have to be patient—and believe it'll work out OK in the end."

Your Dog, a Believer

That wasn't what Kay wanted to hear. "It's so hard to do nothing and wait," she protested.

"You can keep praying," Mary tried to assure her. "That's not 'doing nothing.' It's voicing your needs to the only One who has power to change things."

Kay sighed wearily. "It even feels like praying is useless." That felt like a dangerous admission, but Kay also felt relieved to have brought her feelings out into the open. She glanced at Mary to see if the revelation had shocked her, but Mary's face registered only compassion and support. "You know how many times I've been on my knees for him, begging God to change Alan's heart and bring him back home, but things just keep getting worse instead of better."

When Alan had finished high school, he decided he didn't need college or help from his parents—not if it came with any type of rules or restrictions. Now he was off on his own, living the "good life"—or so he seemed to think. Kay knew the road filled with parties, drugs, and alcohol was the road many kids take, but that was small consolation. She hoped and prayed Alan wouldn't have to hit rock bottom before he came to his senses.

"I've never felt this hopeless before," Kay confided. "It's a feeling of utter abandonment, and it's scary," she explained as Mary pulled into her driveway to drop her off.

Mary leaned over and hugged her discouraged friend as Kay opened the car door to get out. "Why doesn't anything change?" Kay whispered. A tear splashed on Mary's shoulder.

"It will," Mary said earnestly, squeezing Kay tighter for emphasis. "Don't you give up on Alan—or on God," she urged. "Keep believing. Keep talking. Keep the faith. Someday you'll see that you haven't been abandoned or forgotten."

Kay walked sullenly up the path to the front door with the same knot in her stomach and the same heavy heart she'd lived with for months now. Did she dare to hope that Mary was right? Could she believe even when she felt so helpless and alone?

She walked inside to find her husband asleep in his

recliner, a golf game playing loudly on TV. This was Phil's typical pose for a Saturday afternoon, but something wasn't quite right about this picture. She gently nudged her husband till he awoke, then kissed his forehead.

"How was your day?" Phil asked with a lazy smile.

"OK, I guess. We talked about Alan most of the time. It was good to have someone to talk to." Kay suddenly stopped and looked around the room. "Speaking of someone to talk to, where's Jesse?"

Kay's family had always teased her about how she talked to Jesse, her brown and white miniature rat terrier. She regularly carried on a full, albeit one-sided, conversation with her beloved dog.

"I don't know," Phil replied, yawning. "He's got to be around here somewhere."

"He should've been out here by now." Kay had assumed the little dog would be with Phil—in his customary position on the back of the recliner, pink belly curled around the top of Phil's head. But no matter what, Jesse always greeted her when she came home, jumping and barking as if he hadn't seen her in months, even when she'd only been gone for a couple of hours.

"Jesse," Kay called. She continued calling his name, checking all of his favorite haunts before she started searching the house with a new sense of urgency. A mixture of dread and panic rose in her heart. *This isn't normal*, she thought. *Something bad must have happened.*

"Jesse!" Kay called worriedly. "When did you last see him?" she asked Phil, who had joined her search.

"I guess I haven't seen him all afternoon," Phil said, suddenly looking miserable. "But I can't imagine where he could have gone or what sort of trouble he could get into around here," he added hopefully.

They had only been looking for a couple of minutes when they first heard the bark. It was muffled, but they recognized it immediately as Jesse's.

"Where is that coming from?" Kay asked, concerned and puzzled. Then she heard Jesse bark again. It wasn't loud, but it was definitely him. At least he was alive and somewhere nearby. Kay felt a little better. But where was he?

Your Dog, a Believer

Was he stuck somewhere—in the fireplace, under a bed? Could something have fallen on him and injured him so that he couldn't get back to them? A jumble of half-formed questions and irrational fears tumbled through her mind as she ran frantically through the house, checking closets, bathrooms, nooks, and crannies—anywhere a little dog could possibly be. Again they heard the bark.

This time it clicked: "The intercom!" Kay and Phil cried in unison.

"He's in the shop!" Phil hollered. "I must have locked him in when I came in . . . over four hours ago!" Kay and Phil both ran out the back door toward the shop like lifeguards taking off for a big rescue.

Upon retiring, Phil had set up a woodworking shop just behind their house. He'd always loved working with his hands, and although at first he'd intended only to make things for friends and family, he now had a small business. The intercom system between the shop and the house made it easy for Kay to talk to Phil even when he was working. She could call him over for lunch or give him a phone message.

The intercoms also had proven a fun game for the grand-kids. They talked back and forth as if on CB radios. Kay often laughed when she heard a "Ten-four, good buddy," or an "Over and out" from the speaker. But how was it that they were now hearing Jesse over the intercom? It didn't make sense, but that didn't stop Kay from racing to Jesse's side in response to his cries for help.

As Kay and Phil passed the shop's window, they were astounded at what they saw: Jesse was standing up on Phil's chair. He rested one front paw on the desk, but with the other, he was pressing the call button on the intercom while he tirelessly barked out his plea to be found. They had known Jesse was smart: he could shake hands or bark on command. But how had he figured out the intercom system? They were amazed at the ingenuity of their little dog. Even more, Kay marveled at the persistence and faith Jesse had demonstrated after being trapped alone for many hours. How long had he barked into thin air? Why did he keep barking when there was no response for so long?

When Kay and Phil burst through the door, Jesse jumped down and ran to greet them. He jumped into Kay's open arms and licked her face with gratitude and relief.

"Good dog," Kay repeated, hugging Jesse tightly and kissing the brown spot on his head. "You know, Phil, Jesse knew we would rescue him." With tears in her eyes, she continued. "All he had to do was make sure we could hear his voice—he knew that would be enough for us to keep searching until we found him."

Phil nodded his agreement. Then, lightening the mood, he added, "You rescued him all right; I haven't seen you run like that since college." Kay slugged her husband playfully on the shoulder.

That night before bed, Kay prayed a prayer of thankfulness for having Jesse safe at home again. She scratched the little dog behind his ears, then she began praying for her son—the same prayer she had offered up a thousand times before. But now she had a new assurance that God was listening. The feeling of aloneness and abandonment that had weighed so heavily on her heart just hours before was gone. In its place was peace.

Jesse had never given up believing she would rescue him, even when it seemed no one heard him and no one came. New confidence and faith welled up in Kay's heart. She wouldn't give up either. She believed God heard her prayers and cared about her and about Alan. She would never stop praying and believing.

It would be enough.

6

Your Dog, a Companion

I even know when a little sparrow
falls to the ground. And you're
much more valuable than
that. I've engraved you on
the palms of My hands. I
personally know you and
have counted the very hairs
of your head. Take comfort:
you're never alone. Surely I am
always with you.

Forever yours,
Your God and Friend

—FROM MATTHEW 10:29–31; ISAIAH 49:16;
MATTHEW 28:20

Everyone needs a companion. Even when it's not so easy to admit that we do—when we act as though we've got it all together or when we think we don't need anyone or anything—God knows what we need. Sometimes our companions are other human beings, but many times they're not.

Our most loyal companions just might be our dogs. They may not be able to mow the yard or wash the dishes, but they are roommates that help make our houses into homes. And it's those unquantifiable gifts that make them essential to our everyday lives.

Dogs unquestionably do more for us than many people are willing to admit. Although they can't speak to us in words, they most assuredly speak to us loudly in the little things they do for us from day to day.

When your dog faithfully gives you that early morning wake-up call, he's saying that you are needed. When she enthusiastically barks and jumps to greet you each time you come home, she's shouting, "I missed you. I'm glad you're back!" When she's never too busy to snuggle on the couch when you're alone at night, she's letting you know that you're loved and valued.

Today take a moment to appreciate your dog—even though he hasn't once taken out the trash. The little things dogs do to enrich our lives make them more than just pets; they're bona fide, loving companions.

No matter how **little** money and
how **few** possessions you own,
having a dog makes you **rich**.

Louis Sabin

Jane chafed at the thought
of needing anyone's help—
especially her mother's
"security blanket," this
little brown beagle.

Comforts of Home 6

"Mom, I've already told you, I don't need a pet," Jane hollered over her shoulder as she carried another suitcase to the car.

"It will be a companion," retorted Jane's mother with resolve. "I just can't send you off totally alone."

"A companion, a pet, a dog, a puppy—it doesn't matter what you call it; I don't want it." Jane tried again to assert her independence as she walked back up the steps to the house where she had lived all her life.

"Listen, Jane, you're still my little girl, even if you are going off to college in the big city." Her mother tried again, pleading. "Take the puppy as a favor to me."

Jane chafed at the thought of needing anyone's help— especially her mother's "security blanket," this little brown beagle. Jane had always possessed an independent spirit, and she was excited by the prospect of making it on her own at New York University after spending her freshman year at a smaller school in her hometown. But Jane also knew that her parents had doted on their only child and would undoubtedly miss their daily contact even more than she would. They had attended every concert, program, and sporting event Jane had ever participated in, video camera in hand. Now Jane suspected that her mother would stop at nothing short of actually getting into one of Jane's suitcases to make sure her only child would be safe. *That would never do*, Jane thought to herself with a smile. Taking the dog seemed like a good compromise.

"OK, OK, I'll take her." Jane relented. She couldn't help feeling a little guilty about leaving her parents in that big, old house all alone, even if the city was just three hours away from their home in upstate New York. *What will they do without me to worry about or wait up for on the weekends?* Jane thought as her mother placed the puppy in her hands.

The creature was tiny and delicate. Jane laughed to

herself at the idea that this puppy could do anything for her—what could a little dog like this protect her from? *She is cute*, Jane thought. *But she looks like a lot of work.* Jane really didn't want the responsibility. Truth be known, she wanted to feel free, and this seemed like a burden.

"What will you name her?" her mom asked, smiling through tears.

Jane looked away, struggling to keep from being engulfed by her mother's emotion. "Give me a break, Mom," she protested, gazing down at the little puppy in her arms. "I just resigned myself to keeping the little critter—I'll think of a name for her once I get settled in."

Jane finished cramming her belongings into the last inches of space in her car just as her dad arrived home from work. He got out of his car with a questioning look on his face. That's when Jane realized her parents had collaborated about the dog. "The answer is yes," Jane said, putting on an exaggerated air of self-sacrifice. "I'm taking the puppy."

Her dad smiled, looked relieved, and embraced Jane. "Are you ready to go?" he asked, still holding her tight.

"I was born ready," Jane kidded gently, sensing the deep emotion of her big-hearted dad.

He held her at arm's length, then addressed her mother: "Molly, our little girl is all grown up. She's going to do just fine on her own."

The three embraced one more time and kissed each other good-bye. Everyone cried, but Jane's tears of sadness mingled with tears of excitement. She climbed into her car with her new puppy, backed out of the driveway, and watched her parents in the rearview mirror, waving until she had turned the corner.

Her first night in the empty little apartment she'd picked out with her parents during the summer was both thrilling and strangely lonely. She could hardly wait to begin her new independent life. While she felt a little nervous about living off campus and not knowing anyone, she knew she would make friends as soon as classes began. After sorting through the suitcases and boxes until almost midnight and taking the puppy out for what felt like thousands of housebreaking sessions, she placed her in the kitchen in the kennel her mom had bought. Then she made a bed for herself by layering blankets on the carpet in the bedroom.

But Jane couldn't sleep. The incessant, plaintive whimpering from the kitchen was heartrending. *My "companion" is the one who's lonely, not me,* Jane thought smugly, and she reluctantly brought the puppy to the bedroom. As they snuggled together on the blankets, Jane had to admit that the warmth she felt from the little animal was soothing. They both fell asleep quickly and slept peacefully together until the sun crept through the window.

The tiny beagle woke Jane early, nibbling on her pajamas with little puppy teeth. Jane reluctantly stretched and threw on some clothes so she could take her out and avoid an accident in the new apartment. She set out some food for the little dog and then was ready to get on with her first order of business—buying furniture with the money her parents had given her. Jane took her time getting ready but still was fully dressed and out the door before the furniture stores were open. She decided to find a restaurant nearby for some breakfast.

As she walked into a small coffee shop at the corner

of her block, the young man behind the counter smiled warmly and took her order. By the time Jane had finished her breakfast, she had learned that he was a student at NYU and lived off campus nearby. He had also complimented her on her eyes, causing her to blush and fumble gracelessly for a suitable reply. She finally settled on "Thank you," then excused herself, saying she had a lot to do.

At a furniture store three blocks down, it didn't take her long to choose a red, slipcovered couch and a wooden and wrought-iron bed with a matching dresser and nightstand. They were totally different from the white wicker in her bedroom at home but seemed to fit her new life just right. She made arrangements to have the furniture delivered that afternoon, then headed back to her apartment. She'd check on the puppy and wait for her purchases to arrive.

Just before she'd given up on the furniture arriving that day, the deliverymen knocked on her door. They moved the bulky pieces up five flights of stairs and into her apartment with surprising ease.

Jane plopped down on her new sofa, excited to call her

mom with the news of her day. But thoughts of the dog stopped her—Mom would ask first about how the puppy was getting along and about what she had named her. Jane suddenly realized she hadn't seen or heard from the pup since the deliverymen had left.

"Here, little doggy," she called, having still not taken the time to come up with a name.

Silence.

Jane quickly searched the small apartment. *She must have escaped when the door was open,* Jane surmised. "I knew this dog was a bad idea," she mumbled as she headed out the door to search the halls and knock on doors.

The puppy was not in the hallway. No one answered when she knocked on the first couple of doors. An old woman answered the third but hadn't seen the dog, and a man's voice hollered at her to go away when she knocked on the fourth. Jane braced herself to knock at the final apartment on the hall, but to her surprise the door slowly opened before she knocked.

"Shhhh!" warned a low voice, a finger pressed against a

startling familiar face she couldn't immediately place. Then she saw recognition dawn in the dark eyes and the same warm smile she remembered from the coffee shop that morning.

Jane was clueless—and speechless. "What . . . how . . . ," she managed to stammer.

That smile again. "I heard you making your way down the hall knocking on doors. I didn't want you to wake up Molly—she's sleeping—got all tuckered out from her little adventure."

"Molly?" Jane asked once she managed to stop her mouth from hanging open. "Who's Molly?"

"Well, I'm assuming she's your puppy." He moved aside and gestured toward the tiny beagle puppy curled up peacefully on a couch pillow. This guy's smile just got better and better. He was obviously amused and enjoying her confusion. "But then again, I'm sure that's not her name. I've been calling her Molly. It seemed to suit her."

"That's my mom's name!" Jane replied, eyes wide in disbelief. "It's perfect! But how did she . . . how did you . . ."

"She was sitting at my doorstep when I came home from work this afternoon," he explained kindly. "I figured she had escaped from somewhere and someone would come looking for her."

"My name's Scott," he said as he scooped up the puppy and handed her to Jane. "You escaped this morning without telling me yours."

"Oh—Jane. Hi." She smiled, blushed, then added, "Thanks for taking care of her. I'm sorry for any inconvenience."

"No inconvenience at all. I love dogs and have been thinking of getting one myself," Scott said with that grin that was beginning to make Jane feel weak in the knees. "Everyone needs a companion."

As Jane turned to leave, Scott offered, "I'm free tomorrow if you'd like me to show you around town."

Jane accepted the invitation eagerly—not too eagerly, she hoped. She said good-bye to Scott and went home. Holding her puppy close, she whispered a sincere thank you into Molly's small, floppy ear. Then, as she snuggled with her little dog on her new red sofa, she dialed her parents' number. *Maybe,* Jane thought with a smile, *a companion isn't such a bad idea after all.*

7

Your Dog, a Giver

No greater love has ever been shown than when someone willingly gives his life for a friend. That's the kind of love I have for you. I am your Good Shepherd, willing to lay down My life to save you. It's rare for someone to give his life for another. But what's truly incredible is that I gave Myself for you before you loved Me or even knew Me. Now you have My perfect example of sacrificial love. Even so, you should follow My example and give your life for others.

Loving you at all costs,

Jesus

—FROM JOHN 15:13; 10:11; ROMANS 5:7–8; 1 JOHN 3:16

Have you ever witnessed a pure act of compassion, a true example of sacrificial love?

If you've ever been at the right time and place to view such a gift, you know it will be forever etched in your memory and in your heart.

We've all heard stories of the dog that ran back into the burning building to save a child or who placed himself between a baby and a poisonous snake, willing to take the bite to save the little one. Dogs are famous for their faithfulness to the ones they love.

Dogs sometimes remind us of the purity in loving actions. They don't weigh the odds or think about what would be best for them; they simply react, and in

that reaction we are privileged to glimpse true
loyalty.

Jesus said, "Greater love has no one than this,
that he lay down his life for his friends" (John 15:13).
And even though He was talking about human love,
that truth is often exemplified in our dogs. They love us
totally and completely, without reservation. Sometimes
they give comfort, sometimes joy, or laughter, or even
tears. But always they give us the gift of love, even at
the cost of their own well-being.

God loves us that much too. His act of sending His Son to die for us is the ultimate example of sacrificial love, and once we've
caught a glimpse of that powerful love,
we can never be the same.

A dog is the **only** thing on
this earth that loves **you**
more than he loves himself.

Josh Billings

Sadie was always on call, always
ready to get up and go
whenever Ellen needed her,
eager to guide and protect.

Greater Love

A sick sense of dread gripped Ellen's heart. She could feel the unmistakable stickiness of blood on Sadie's foreleg and knew the guide dog was injured and in pain. Still, Sadie valiantly struggled to lead her master home safely, although slowed by a noticeable limp. Would Sadie's strength hold out long enough?

"Tom!" Ellen cried frantically when she and Sadie finally made it the two blocks to their own driveway after the terrible accident. Ellen heard the front door bang and the sound of bare feet approaching through soft grass. She sensed her husband's presence and smelled his cologne even before she felt his gentle hands on her arms or heard his concerned voice.

"Ellen, you're hurt," Tom said, inspecting her bloody hands.

Ellen collapsed into Tom's strong arms. "No, but Sadie is."

"What happened?" They both knelt by the panting dog now sprawled, exhausted and bleeding, on the grass of home and safety.

"I couldn't hear them until it was too late . . . boys on bicycles," Ellen gasped. "They must have come around the corner just as we started to cross the street . . . going way too fast . . . Tom, there was nothing we could do!"

"They didn't even stop to help you?" Ellen could hear disbelief and anger in Tom's voice.

"Sadie knocked me down," Ellen continued breathlessly. "Back onto the sidewalk. She saved me, Tom—but she couldn't save herself." Ellen sniffed loudly.

"They were so close, I could feel the wind from their bikes as they passed by," she continued, her chin quivering with emotion. "It was terrifying! Then I heard a sickening thump, and Sadie yelped in pain . . . I knew she had sacrificed herself for me . . ." Ellen sobbed, finally allowing the fear and feelings of helplessness to spill over her thin veneer of control. "Oh, Tom, how bad is she? Is she . . . is she going to be OK?"

"I don't know," Tom admitted, turning his attention to the heroic dog. "Let's get her to the vet's office fast."

Ellen crawled into the backseat of the car. She could hear Tom strain with exertion as he lifted the big dog gently onto the seat beside her. She cradled Sadie's head tenderly in her lap as Tom left to get his shoes and lock up the house.

"You're a good girl," Ellen whispered soothingly. "You've been the best guide dog and friend I could ever have wanted." Hot tears stung Ellen's eyes, and she buried her face in Sadie's fur. "Thank you. Thank you for everything you've ever done for me—for everything you've given."

Ellen desperately hoped this wouldn't be good-bye.

She remembered how small and frightening her world had been before Sadie had "rescued" her more than eight years ago. Since then Sadie had been more than Ellen's eyes; she had been her heart.

Ellen loved having Sadie with her. The dog had seen Ellen through countless trials and difficulties. She had guided her through town; through grocery stores and malls; through Disney World and many other family vacations; and through her days as a teacher, wife, and mom.

She was proud of the magnificent way Sadie operated. People were inspired when they saw the beautiful, intelligent dog at work. Sadie was always on call, always ready to get up and go whenever Ellen needed her, eager to guide and protect.

Even at rest, Sadie had always been perfect—sitting patiently, not distracted by other things or people, and always gentle and patient with excitable children. German shepherds were known for their strong character, their uncanny intelligence, and their faithfulness. Sadie had exemplified all the best traits of her breed every day of her life.

Now, as Sadie groaned softly and gently licked her own blood from Ellen's hands, Ellen couldn't help but note the irony: Sadie's blood was on her hands. She felt miserably guilty and responsible for what had happened. Why had she taken her walking on the busy city streets so soon? Sadie had only resumed her guiding role a few days ago, after recovering from eye surgery. But Ellen had been so glad to have her back and just wanted to get back to normal. They had always enjoyed their evening walks together. Now she had to face the possibility that things might never be normal again.

Tom was back. She heard his seat belt click shut and the whine of the mirror moving. She guessed he was making sure he could check on her and Sadie as he drove. His care and concern warmed Ellen's heart. But even those thoughts reinforced her feelings of guilt.

It had been Tom who had first broached the subject that maybe it was time for Ellen to think about getting a new guide dog. Ellen had flatly refused to listen to his gentle suggestions that the ten-year-old dog's growing health problems were slowing her down and making her work difficult. Ellen didn't want to think of Sadie's growing old. She didn't ever want to give up the smooth and wonderful working relationship—not to mention the close personal bond—with this wonderful dog. So what if Sadie wasn't as fast as she used to be? She was still far faster than Ellen was, and that was enough. A little arthritis? Even Ellen had a little arthritis, but she kept going, and so would Sadie.

Sure, there had been the eye problems. But dogs of any age could get eye infections, right? And after the surgery Sadie could see fine.

Tom was silent as they drove, but she could feel his eyes on her—boring into her. He didn't say it now, and she appreciated that, but he didn't have to. She knew what he was thinking.

Had she missed the signs that it was time for Sadie to retire? Had she waited too long? Would Sadie have to pay the ultimate price because Ellen had selfishly refused to see the handwriting on the wall and let her faithful friend and guide go?

She gently kissed Sadie's head as Tom stopped the car, got out, and opened the back door. "Hang in there, girl," she encouraged. Ellen winced when Sadie yipped as Tom picked her up. "Careful!" Ellen admonished. "It's OK, Sadie, the doctor is here. You'll be OK," she promised.

After more than one insufferable hour in the waiting room, the doctor emerged from treating Sadie. "She'll be OK, Ellen," he announced. "I promise."

Ellen clapped her hands and laughed with relief. Tom put his hands on her shoulders and squeezed supportively.

"She'll need surgery to repair damage to her shoulder and set that broken leg, so she'll have to stay here for a few days. But she should heal just fine."

"Thank you, Doctor." Ellen reached out to touch the doctor's arm appreciatively. She heard him pull up a chair to face hers and knew he had something serious to say. She was convinced Tom and the doctor were communicating silently with their eyes and facial expressions. It was unnerving to be left out of the loop when Sadie was her dog.

"We have to talk about Sadie's future," the doctor said in a calm, nonconfrontational tone. "She won't heal as fast as she did when she was young," he warned. "She'll have to stay off her feet for a few weeks." Ellen nodded. "And you'll have to get along without her for even longer than that—like after the eye surgery."

Your Dog, a Giver

He paused, and Ellen remembered the difficult adjustment that had been. It had meant a return to the difficult days with a cane before Sadie had come along. The cane didn't come when she called it and was easily misplaced. Stairs were frightening, and people seemed to shy away from her with the cane rather than being drawn to Sadie's friendly personality. Ellen had hated that time, but she knew she could get through it if she had to. And now she had to.

Suddenly she knew what she needed to do. Sadie had sacrificed herself for Ellen time and time again, and now it was time for Ellen to return the favor. An act of pure, sacrificial love had brought about Sadie's injury. Now Ellen's love for her dog made this decision unavoidable . . . but no less difficult.

The doctor cleared his throat to speak again, but Ellen spoke first. "It's OK. Sadie can take all the time she needs to recuperate and rest," she announced. "It's time for Sadie to retire. She has served my interests well for eight years. Now it's time I served hers."

Tom put his arms around her. He and the doctor both

talked at once. "She'll always be a treasured part of the family—," Tom said.

"You can apply for another guide dog immediately," the doctor was saying. "It won't be the same, but—"

"No one could ever replace Sadie," Tom agreed.

Surprisingly, Ellen felt good about her decision. She knew it was the right one for Sadie, the dog who exemplified faithfulness, loyalty, and sacrificial love. Ellen suddenly began to relish the thought of her beloved dog being able to relax, lazing around the house doing normal dog things. Then she laughed at the thought of Sadie ever being normal. She was— and always would be—a most extraordinary dog.